I0813144

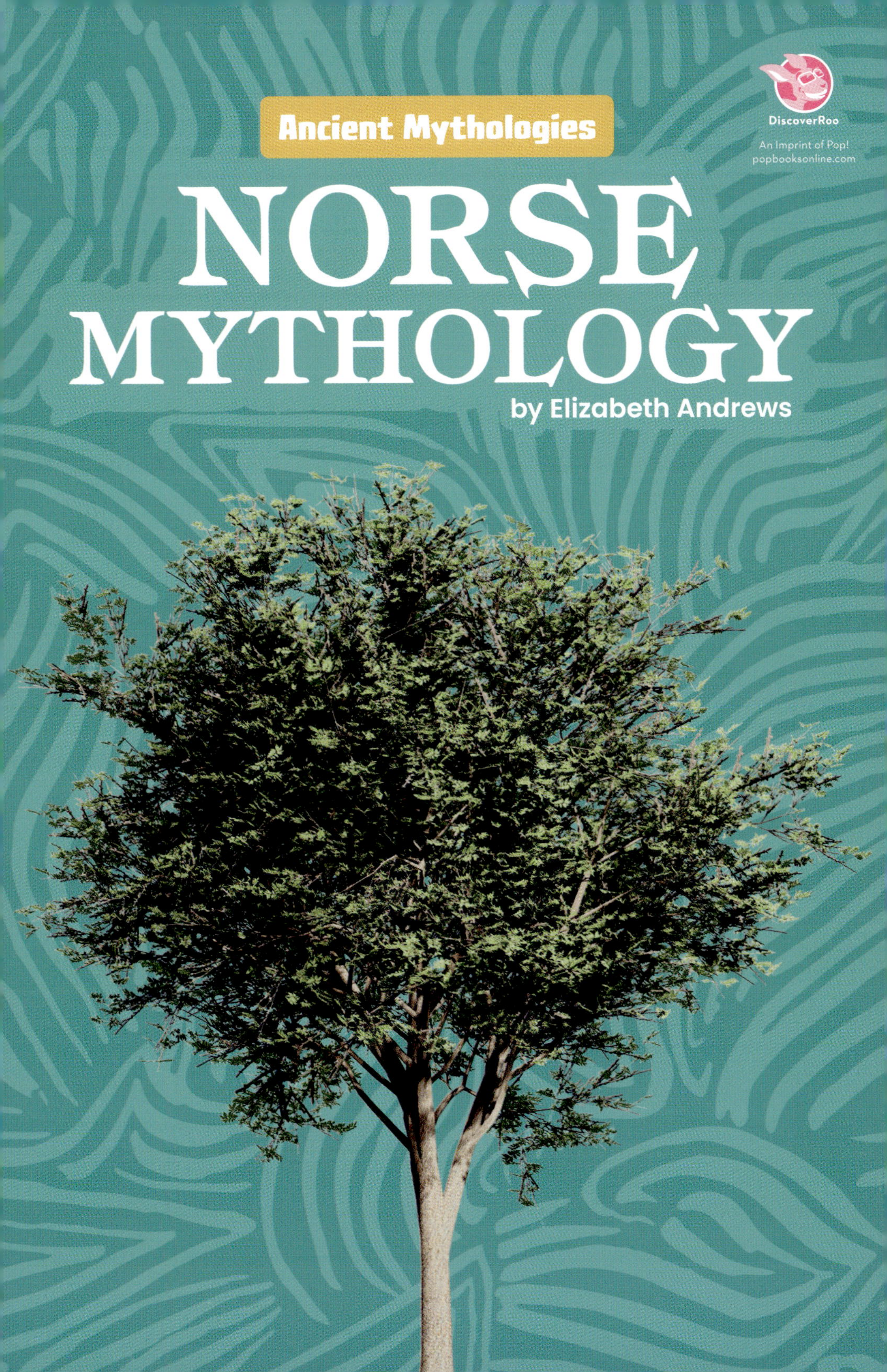

Ancient Mythologies
NORSE MYTHOLOGY
by Elizabeth Andrews
DiscoverRoo
An Imprint of Pop!
popbooksonline.com

WELCOME TO DiscoverRoo!

This book is filled with videos, puzzles, games, and more! Scan the QR codes* while you read, or visit the website below to make this book pop.

popbooksonline.com/norse-myth

abdobooks.com

Published by Pop!, a division of ABDO, PO Box 398166, Minneapolis, Minnesota 55439.

Printed in the United States of America, North Mankato, Minnesota.

102024
012025

Cover Photo: Wikimedia Commons

Interior Photos: Alamy Stock Photos, Getty Images, Shutterstock Images, Wikimedia Commons

Editor: Krissy Sterling

Series Designer: Colleen McLaren

Library of Congress Control Number: 2024938629

Publisher's Cataloging-in-Publication Data

Names: Andrews, Elizabeth, author.

Title: Norse mythology / by Elizabeth Andrews

Description: Minneapolis, Minnesota : Pop!, 2025 | Series: Ancient mythologies | Includes online resources and index

Identifiers: ISBN 9781098247058 (lib. bdg.) | ISBN 9781098247614 (ebook)

Subjects: LCSH: Mythology--Juvenile literature. | Mythology, Norse--Juvenile literature. | Gods, Norse--Juvenile literature. | Deities--Juvenile literature. | Mythology, Scandinavian--Juvenile literature.

Classification: DDC 293.1--dc23

*Scanning QR codes requires a web-enabled smart device with a QR code reader app and a camera.

TABLE OF CONTENTS

CHAPTER 1

LAND OF FIRE AND ICE

Before the world existed, there was only the land of ice in the north and the land of fire in the south. There was a gap where the ice and fire met. The gap was filled with huge clouds of steam.

WATCH A VIDEO HERE!

The gap was called Ginnungagap. It was completely dark and silent.

Some ancient Norse people lived in Iceland. There they would have seen volcanoes surrounded by ice. That might have inspired the mythological gap between ice and fire.

Giants had heads as hard as rocks and feet of ice.

A powerful giant emerged from the steam. His name was Ymir, and he was evil. A cow formed from melting ice. She fed Ymir her milk. Ymir rested in the gap. As he did, his sweat formed other frost giants.

The cow licked salt from stones, revealing the first Norse god named Buri. He was good and had a warm heart. Buri had three important grandchildren. They were Odin, Vili, and Ve.

Buri's son was named Borr.

Giants and gods did not get along. Odin and his brothers decided they must kill the evil giant Ymir. After slaying Ymir, the brothers dragged his body to the bottom of the empty gap.

The hatred between gods and giants would lead to a war.

Odin, Vili, and Ve used his body to create the earth, seas, and skies in a **realm** called Midgard. They also made the sun, moon, and stars with sparks from the land of fire.

Odin and his brothers visited Midgard. They found an ash tree and an elm tree. Odin breathed life into the trees. Vili touched the trees and made them wise. Ve gave them the ability to see, speak, and hear. He shaped them into humans. From a realm called Asgard, the gods watched over humans. The realms were connected by a giant tree called Yggdrasil.

The first humans were named Askr and Embla.

Vikings were warriors from northern Europe. They attacked villages and stole treasure.

Nearly every society has a creation myth. Myths are stories that often involve gods and **supernatural** events. They are not always based in fact. Myths helped people make sense of the world around them. Norse myths come from the people who lived in **Scandinavia** long ago. Some of them were Vikings.

CHAPTER 2

NORSE GODS AND GODDESSES

There are two types of gods in Norse mythology. The Aesir are gods known for their fighting and warfare. The Vanir are gods known for their connection to nature and witchcraft. The Aesir had more power over the world. They are also more well-known.

LEARN MORE HERE!

The goddess Freya rides a chariot pulled by Norwegian forest cats. They are bigger than house cats.

YGGDRASIL

Asgard
Land of the Aesir gods
Vanaheim
Land of the Vanir gods
Midgard
Land of humans
Jotunheim
Land of giants
Niflheim
Land of the dead

The Aesir gods live in Asgard. It is a huge **fortress** set so high on cliffs that it disappears in the clouds. The Vanir gods live in Vanaheim. Both **realms** have many halls for the gods and chosen people to live. Asgard is connected to Midgard by a rainbow bridge.

YGGDRASIL

Yggdrasil is the world tree of the Norse people. There are nine realms in Yggdrasil. At the top is Asgard, the realm of the Aesir. Humans live in the middle of the tree in the realm called Midgard. The deepest roots of the tree reach the realm of death. An evil dragon lives there.

The ravens Hugin and Munin work for the god Odin.

Odin uses a spear called Gungnir. It always hits its target.

Odin is the ruler of the gods. He is also the god of wisdom and war. Odin watches over the world from his high seat. Odin is powerful. He can see the future and perform magic spells. Odin is married to Frigg. She is the goddess of love and marriage. Frigg can also see the future.

Thor is Odin's son. He is the god of the sky, thunder, and **agriculture**. Thor possesses an important tool, the hammer called Mjollnir. This hammer was specially crafted by dwarfs. No matter where Thor throws it, the hammer always comes back to him. He uses his powers and hammer to protect the gods and humans from giants.

Thor drives a chariot pulled by goats.

CHAPTER 3

LOKI THE TRICKSTER

Loki is another famous Norse god. He is a trickster. Loki is the child of a god and a giant. He lives in Asgard but sometimes takes the side of giants. Loki can change his shape and **gender**. This is how he plays so many tricks on gods and giants.

EXPLORE LINKS HERE!

Loki is mentioned more in Norse mythology than any other god.

Loki had three children with a giantess. Hel was the goddess of death. Half of her body was a beautiful woman. The other half was a **corpse**. Fenrir was a wolf. At first, he was raised by gods. But he grew too big and powerful. The gods used magical chains to contain him. Jörmungand was a sea serpent so giant his body circled the world. The serpent was Thor's worst enemy.

Since Loki could turn into a woman, he gave birth to his own children.

Before he died, Balder had a dream that his life was in danger.

Odin and Frigg had a son named Balder. He was nearly perfect, but his fate was **doomed**. Frigg tried to protect him. She traveled the **realms** and made everything in the world promise to do him no harm. Many gods liked to throw things at Balder and watch them bounce off.

Snake venom dripped endlessly on Loki's head while he was tied to the rocks.

Loki knew about Frigg's protection. But he discovered she never made mistletoe promise not to hurt Balder. Loki tricked Balder's blind brother, Höd, into throwing mistletoe at Balder. The mistletoe struck him in the chest. Balder died. Odin and the other gods punished Loki by tying him to rocks.

Freya is the Vanir goddess of love and **fertility**. She owned the most beautiful necklace in the world called Brísingamen. It was made by dwarfs. Loki turned into a fly to break into Freya's home. He stole the necklace. Heimdall, the protector of the gods, fought Loki and won the necklace back for Freya.

Dwarfs existed before humans.

CHAPTER 4

RAGNAROK

According to Norse mythology, the world as we know it will end. There will be a battle between the gods called Ragnarok. The gods are always preparing for the final battle.

Odin keeps a team of female warriors called Valkyries. They are very beautiful and dress in armor. Valkyries offer

COMPLETE AN ACTIVITY HERE!

protection to warriors during battle. When a battle is over, Valkyries look over all the dead fighters. If a fighter is worthy, they bring his spirit to the hall of Valhalla in Asgard. There, Odin trains the warriors for Ragnarok.

FREYA

Freya also selects warriors to bring the realm of the Vanir after battles. She brought them to a hall called Sessrumnir.

Valkyries may also ride wolves and boars.

The beginning of Ragnarok will be signaled by the trembling of Yggdrasil. The wolves who chase the sun and moon through the sky will finally catch them. The world will plunge into darkness.

While the world turns dark, mountains will crumble, and trees will fall. All the monsters the gods kept contained will be freed, including the giant wolf, Fenrir, and the god Loki. Once free, Loki will build an army of dead souls and giants to fight the Aesir. Odin will lead the Aesir and the warriors from Valhalla.

Valhalla is a beautiful palace with a roof made of warrior shields.

The wolves who chase the sun and moon are Fenrir's children.

During the final battle, most of the gods will die. Odin will get swallowed by Fenrir. His son will kill Fenrir in **revenge**. Thor will defeat his worst enemy, the serpent Jörmungand, but die from its venom. Odin's and Thor's sons will survive Ragnarok. Balder will come back from

Loki will have frost and fire giants in his army.

the land of the dead. The world will begin anew under his protection.

Norse mythology explains an ancient peoples' everyday hopes and fears. The stories have inspired many modern works of art and entertainment.

MAKING CONNECTIONS

TEXT-TO-SELF

Which Norse god were you most interested in? Please explain your answer.

TEXT-TO-TEXT

Have you read about a different ancient mythology? If so, what did it have in common with Norse mythology?

TEXT-TO-WORLD

Many ancient mythologies have stories about tricksters such as the Norse god Loki. With the help of an adult, look up a trickster from a different mythology online. Write a few sentences about how they are similar to or different from Loki.

GLOSSARY

agriculture — the science or activity of farming.

corpse — a dead body.

doomed — certain to fail, die, or be destroyed.

fertility — a woman's ability to have children.

fortress — a strong and permanent place of safety.

gender — a word commonly used to describe whether someone is male or female.

realm — an area.

revenge — the act of giving punishment in payment for a wrong that has been done.

Scandinavia — part of northern Europe including Norway, Sweden, Denmark, and Iceland.

supernatural — having to do with forces beyond what is natural.

INDEX

DiscoverRoo!
ONLINE RESOURCES

This book is filled with videos, puzzles, games, and more! Scan the QR codes* while you read, or visit the website below to make this book pop.

popbooksonline.com/norse-myth

*Scanning QR codes requires a web-enabled smart device with a QR code reader app and a camera.